Our human ancestors walked upright on the open plains. Chimpanzees were more at home with life in the forests. They have long arms, fingers, and toes for reaching and clinging to branches. Chimps use their hands to climb through trees and usually walk on all fours. They can also use their hands to make simple tools and use them.

Chimp talk

Chimpanzees have complicated social lives and their own language of signs and sounds. Given the chance, a chimp can even learn ways of communicating with humans. In this book you will discover how chimps live together, and how these animals spend their days.

This chimpanzee looks both relaxed and aware of its surroundings.

Brainpower

Chimpanzees have big brains and are very intelligent. Chimps can solve tricky practical problems. They learn from their friends, so different groups of chimps deal with the same problems in different ways. This is what makes chimpanzees so unpredictable, and why their behavior is so fascinating.

Living together

All chimpanzees live in groups of 15 to 120 animals. Each community is based on related males. The group lives in an area called the home range.

The chimps in the community use the home range in different ways. An adult female has her own special part of the range, which she shares with her young. Female chimps often meet to feed at fruiting trees and sometimes form special friendships.

Adult males roam all over the home range, often in parties of three to six. They are more sociable than females, but they are always arguing over who's boss. There is a definite pecking order, or hierarchy, in chimp society, especially among males. The pecking order

A group of male chimps is going for a bathe. The chimp in the water is probably the gang's boss.

ANIMAL FAMILIES
Chimpanzees

General Editor
Tim Harris

BROWN BEAR BOOKS

Published by Brown Bear Books Ltd

4877 N. Circulo Bujia
Tucson, AZ 85718
USA

and

First Floor
9-17 St. Albans Place
London N1 0NX

© 2012 Brown Bear Books Ltd

ISBN: 978-1-78121-001-7

Managing Editor: Tim Harris
Designer: Lynne Lennon
Picture Manager: Sophie Mortimer
Art Director: Jeni Child
Production Director: Alastair Gourlay
Editorial Director: Lindsey Lowe
Children's Publisher: Anne O'Daly

Library of Congress Cataloging-in-Publication Data available upon request.

Publisher's note to educators and parents: Our editors have carefully reviewed the websites that appear on p. 31 to ensure that they are suitable for students. Many websites change frequently, however, and we cannot guarantee that a site's future contents will continue to meet our high standards of quality and educational value. Be advised that students should be closely supervised whenever they access the Internet.

Manufactured in the United States of America

Contents

Introduction

There is something very special about chimpanzees. Every chimp has its own character. It has its own likes and dislikes and can learn many different skills.

Chimps are smart. A chimp can invent a new skill and show it to its friends. Chimpanzees are like us. That is not surprising: They are our nearest living relatives. Chimps and humans are descended from the same ancestors, who lived in Africa several million years ago.

A sleepy young chimp with an older brother or sister and their mother (with the darker face).

changes as young chimps get strong
enough to show how tough they are.
When different parties get together
after a few days apart, there is a noisy
reunion. They shout, scream, hug, and
even threaten each other.

Jostling for position

Male chimpanzees have a complicated
social life. They compete against each
other for status and for females. They
also form alliances to defend the
community and their own position
within it. They usually avoid serious
arguments, but sometimes rival
chimps refuse to back down. They
may grab, kick, and bite each other.

⬆ **A group of two adult females and three young chimpanzees relaxes in the warm sunshine.**

Pushing their luck

As young chimps play with each other, they find out what other chimps like and dislike. They soon discover that they can push some chimps farther than others. They challenge each other and develop their own pecking order. These are useful lessons for the future.

Getting along

Chimpanzees are emotional animals, and they show it. When they meet after a few days apart, there is always a lot of hugging, kissing, and arguing.

Chimpanzee body language is easy for us to understand. A dominant chimp swaggers around with its shoulders hunched and its hair bristling, shaking a broken branch. Meanwhile, a submissive chimp crouches with his back turned, peering fearfully over his shoulder.

Expressive faces

Facial expressions are more difficult for us to understand. An angry chimp clenches his mouth firmly, but a fearful chimp often grins, showing his clenched teeth in a way that looks quite fierce. These are just two of a wide range of expressions. They are backed up by 13 different types of call, each with many variations. Chimps use their expressions and noises to tell each other all kinds of information.

This chimp is grinning with its teeth held tightly together. It is backing down in front of another chimp.

Grooming

When the dust settles after a chimpanzee reunion, they all sit down to groom each other. They use their sensitive fingers to pick off mud, flaking skin, and parasites such as ticks. Offering to groom another chimp is a way of making friends or patching up quarrels.

➲ **A chimp's sensitive fingers pick bits of mud off a friend's fur.**

Sign language

Scientists have tried to teach chimpanzees the sign language used by deaf people. Some chimps are good at this. They have learned the signs for many words and put them together to make simple sentences. They may not be able to talk, but they have other ways of speaking.

Relaxed

Worried

Happy

Frightened

⬆ **These chimpanzees are showing their feelings.**

Time to eat

Chimpanzees will eat almost anything they can digest. Their favorite food is ripe fruit. They also enjoy young leaves, nuts, insects, and meat.

They eat fruit for about four hours a day, usually in the morning. Rain forest trees have fruit at different times of the year. Fruiting trees may be scattered all over the home range, so the community splits up into feeding parties that visit particular trees. Chimps have an amazing ability to remember

An adult chimp relaxes while eating a piece of fruit.

Two chimpanzees run through the forest on their way to a fruiting tree.

when each tree has its fruit. When the chimpanzees set off each morning, they usually know exactly where they are going.

Sharing a feast

When chimps find a good tree, they celebrate by making a great deal of noise. The commotion often draws other chimps to share the feast. A big, heavily laden tree may attract 20 or more. They pluck the fruit with their hands. Unless they are really hungry, they leave the seeds and tough skin. By midday the chimps are ready for a few hours' rest. They feed again in the afternoon, usually on leaves.

Hunting parties

Chimpanzees are not just peaceful fruit eaters. They can be killers too. Some chimps—usually males— organize hunts. Colobus monkeys are favorite targets. A group of males may spot a colobus and climb into position to block its escape. Other chimpanzees drive the monkey into the ambush.

Finding a mate

Mating is very important for chimps. In some groups all the adults mate with each other. In other groups, a dominant male keeps some females for himself.

The swollen pink rump of this female chimp shows that she is ready to breed.

From the age of about 10, a female chimp knows she can win useful friends among the males in a group by mating with them. When she comes into breeding condition every month, she starts getting friendly with high-ranking males. She may mate with several males a day for a week or so, but at this age she cannot become pregnant. As soon as she is able to become pregnant – at the age of about 14 – things start to get really serious.

Jealous males

A male can tell when a female is in breeding condition because her rump swells up like a pink cushion. When a female chimp's rump gets very big, it means she is ready to mate. Now the males become jealous of each other. Sometimes one dominant male tries to keep the female to himself by closely following her, grooming her, and driving away rival males.

➲ **A mom suckles her newborn. Female chimps are pregnant for a little less than eight months before giving birth.**

Sneaky moves

Although dominant male chimps father most of the children in a group, they don't have it all their own way. A lower-ranking male may try to attract a female away from him. If she likes him, they may sneak off together to mate.

Growing up

A mother chimpanzee is pregnant for seven or eight months, and she usually has just one baby at a time. The newborn chimp is quite helpless.

Mom has to hold the baby against her as she moves around. She feeds her baby on her milk and stays close to other mothers or friendly males for protection. Males from other chimp communities sometimes attack their neighbors, and babies are often the first to suffer.

At about six months the young chimp starts riding on the mother's back for a better view of the world.

Grown-ups' food

About this time the young chimp tries eating solid foods. The mother has to show the young chimp what it can and cannot eat, since it has no idea. By the age of about four years old the young chimp stops feeding on its mother's milk.

◑ **Young chimps love to play, and nothing is more fun than clambering around in trees.**

It can walk at this age but usually prefers to stay with mom until it is at least five, and often much older.

Baby chimps play all the time. They chase each other around trees, run, and climb. This makes them fit and agile. It also helps them get along with each other. They learn to give and take and to understand the expressions and sounds made by their elders.

⊕ **A baby chimp holds on tight to its mom's fur as it hitches a ride on her back.**

Early learning

Young chimps learn most of what they know by watching the adults in their group. They copy the way they build nests, find food, and use tools. If a young chimp gets it wrong, his or her mother is likely to show them the right way. Teaching is rare among animals, but chimps do it all the time.

Male chimps

By the age of five or six a young male chimp is learning to look after himself. He makes his own sleeping nest and finds most of his own food.

He no longer depends on his mother for everything, and he starts showing an interest in male society. He challenges other young males to trials of strength and starts trailing around after the big adult males. At the age of eight or nine he may be adopted by one adult as an apprentice. Then he starts learning what being a male chimp is all about.

Defending the home range

Chimpanzee society is based on groups of males who are related to each other—fathers, brothers, and cousins.

Groups of male chimps often go looking for trouble. If they find a lone male from another group, they will chase it. Sometimes they will even kill it.

⬆ These two males are having a feast on a good crop of fruit they have found.

They defend their home range against males from other communities. Members of the group squabble over pecking order, but they work well as a team. Since they stay on their home range for life, they know exactly where the borders lie. Since they spend a lot of time near the borders, it is not long before a young male gets to see some serious action.

Border patrols

Most clashes between neighboring groups of males are accidental. They are often settled by shows of strength and loud hooting. Sometimes parties of males go looking for trouble. They creep silently through the forest, watching and listening. If they see their neighbors, they may spy on them for a while. Or they may attack.

Female chimps

A young female chimp stays with her mother for longer than her brothers. When she is about 10 years old, she begins to get interested in the males.

She starts tagging along with parties of males who may mate with her. But she is still too young to have babies. As she gets older, some instinct tells her to find a new home. This is a risky time for a female. She has to leave the community she was born into and move to another. The females who are already there don't like new chimps, although they have all done the same thing themselves.

Luckily the males welcome her. She does her best to encourage them by mating with as many as possible. She still cannot become pregnant.

Having a baby

When a female chimp is about 14 years old, she is ready to have a baby. By this

⬅ **Even an old female chimp, like this one, is treated with respect by other members of her group.**

Mutual grooming is a sign that the females in a chimp community have accepted a female from another group.

time she has claimed a small "core territory" of her own. This territory usually provides enough food for her and her baby.

Gradually she makes friends with the other females. They gather in nursery groups for friendship and to protect their babies against invaders. She is now truly part of her new community.

Social climbing

A newly arrived female has the lowest possible status in the chimp community. All the other females give her a hard time, and she has to live in the parts of the range that nobody else wants. Gradually, she starts to claw her way up. The arrival of even younger females helps, since she can gang up with the other chimps against the newcomers.

Built for the job

A full-grown male chimpanzee has the arm strength of three men, and he is not afraid to use it. Even so, he usually weighs only about 110 pounds (50kg).

This young chimp has a pink face. Adults have black faces.

He is light enough to feed in trees without breaking the branches. Chimps have extralong fingers and toes for hooking around branches, and long arms for reaching across big gaps.

Chimps' eyes face forward to give them stereo vision, so they can see in 3-D like us. This helps chimps judge the distances between branches. They also have good color vision for picking out the glow of ripe fruit among the leaves of trees.

Teeth for chewing and fighting

Chimpanzees' teeth are well suited for eating a wide range of foods, like ours. The teeth are a little bigger than ours and are good for chewing leaves and fruit. The males have extra-long canine teeth that they use when fighting—and those teeth can be lethal.

Fingers and thumbs

A chimpanzee's hand is very like a human hand, with sensitive fingertips and nails instead of sharp claws. A chimp can pinch its thumb and fingers together to grip things, but it cannot bring the tips of its fingers and thumb together.

Chimps are brilliant at swinging beneath the branches of trees.

Knuckle walking

Small monkeys get around in the trees by running along branches. Chimpanzees are too big to do that. Instead, they swing below the branches. Their extralong arms give them a long "stride" so they can move as fast as possible.

Chimps can walk upright, but usually support their weight on the knuckles of their folded fingers. The skin on their knuckles gets very thick and tough.

Chimps' relations

Chimpanzees are apes, part of a large group of mammals called the primates. The primates include all the apes and monkeys—and humans, too.

We are the chimps' closest relatives, along with the other apes: the gibbons, orangutans, and gorillas. The gibbons are the real acrobats of the ape world. Smaller and lighter than chimps, they have even longer, stronger arms. They hurl themselves through the trees with amazing agility and speed. Gibbons live in the forests of Southeast Asia. Like chimps, they mainly eat ripe fruit.

Orangutans are much heavier, but they still spend most of their time in trees. They live on the islands of Sumatra and Borneo in Asia.

The giants of the ape world are the gorillas. A big male can weigh up to 400 pounds (180kg), far too heavy for most branches to bear. Gorillas spend most of their time

An orangutan hangs on to a branch in a forest in Borneo.

⬇ **Bonobos, or pygmy chimpanzees, have slightly longer legs than chimps.**

Bonobos

There are two types of chimps: the chimpanzee and the bonobo. Bonobos are more lightly built and graceful than chimpanzees. They have a different way of life, with communities based on related females rather than males.

eating leaves on the ground. They live in the rain forests of Central Africa, and like orangutans are now very rare.

Chimps' closest relatives

All the information controlling how animals and plants grow is held in a chemical called DNA. This is found in the cells of all living things. The DNA of chimps is very similar to that of humans. Chimpanzees are more closely related to humans than they are to any of the monkeys, for example.

Clever animals

Animal behavior is guided by a set of instructions called instincts. Most animals rely mostly on instinct, but chimps can do more.

Chimps can learn new behaviors—and teach them to other chimps. They have instincts, too, but a lot of their behavior is guided by what they learn, rather than the instincts they inherit. In some ways this makes their life hard, because every chimp has to learn a lot to survive. But it also means they can find new ways of solving problems. Their intelligence helps chimps cope with new situations.

This chimp will use the stick to get termites out of a nest.

Making tools

One way they show this is by using tools. Chimps use stones as hammers to crack nuts. They select the stones carefully to suit the nut they want to break open. Stones are rare in the rain forest, so chimps look after them carefully and even carry them around. They also make tools— such as sponges made of leaves to soak up water and rods to catch burrowing insects. If a tool is not quite right, a chimp will adjust it or make another.

If a chimp is feeling ill, it knows there are leaves it can eat to make it feel better.

Fishing for termites

Termites make tasty, healthy snacks for chimps. The problem is that termites live in tough nests of sun-baked earth, so they are difficult to get at. A chimpanzee solves the problem by making a "fishing rod" from a stick. It slips the rod into a nest entrance and moves it so the termites attack, clamping their jaws into it. The chimp pulls out the rod and eats the termites on it.

Where chimps live

Chimpanzees live in tropical forests. Their main food is fruit, which they climb trees to reach. Every night they make a leafy nest to sleep in.

As well as thick rain forest, chimps can also live in dry woodland or even on grassland as long as there are some trees nearby. Where they live depends on when food is available.

Within the rain forest, trees bear fruit at any time. There is always fruit somewhere, but it can be difficult to find. In the drier woodlands, all the trees come into fruit at about the same time. When that happens, the chimps make the most of it and have a feast. When the fruiting season is over, they go back to the rain forest.

Chimp habitats

The map shows the areas of the world where chimpanzees (shown in red) and bonobos (purple) live. No chimpanzees or bonobos live in the wild outside of Africa.

Some chimpanzees, like these, live in coastal mangrove forests.

This group of chimps is in their favorite habitat—on the branch of a rain forest tree.

Shrinking habitats

A century ago chimpanzees lived all over the tropical green belt of Central and West Africa. It was a patchwork of forest and grassland. The chimps lived wherever they found fruiting trees. Much of the forest has been cut down, so chimps have become much rarer.

People and chimps

In parts of Africa some people eat chimpanzees. The adults are shot and eaten as "bushmeat." Then the orphaned babies are often captured alive.

The orphans are illegally sold to traders and may end up as pets or with traveling entertainers. When they grow too big they are often abandoned. Some chimps are packed into crates and sent to other parts of the world, but most of them will die before they are released.

⬇ **An orphaned chimp being cared for in a rescue center. The animal will be taught how to climb trees and find food.**

Chimps that have lived with people from an early age would find it hard to survive in the wild.

Chimp rescue

There are people who rescue orphaned chimpanzees and give them good homes with other chimps. There are chimpanzee sanctuaries all over the world. The chimps are found in airport luggage and run-down zoos. Often, they cannot find their own food so they can never be returned to the wild.

The luckier ones finish up in zoos and sanctuaries. Some of these are eventually returned to protected areas of forest. Captive-bred chimpanzees are used in some medical laboratories for research into human diseases such as malaria. A few chimps become famous film or TV stars.

Declining numbers

It is particularly sad that our closest relatives are treated so badly because there are fewer than 200,000 chimpanzees remaining in the wild. If people do not start respecting them, they could disappear altogether.

Glossary

ancestors Animals from which chimps have developed over many, many generations.

alliances Friendships that male chimps form with other males.

canine teeth Four pointed teeth at the front of the mouth.

core territory Area a female chimp relies on to provide enough food for her and her offspring.

community A group of chimpanzees whose members share the same area, called a home range.

DNA A chemical that passes features from parents to offspring.

habitat The kind of place where a particular animal lives.

heredity Passing of characteristics from one generation to the next.

hierarchy The pecking order in a community of chimps. Those at the top of the hierarchy are more important than those at the bottom.

instinctive behavior Ability an animal is born with. The animal hasn't learned the ability.

mammal Kind of animal that is warm-blooded and has a backbone. Most are covered with fur. Females have glands that produce milk to feed their young.

nursery group A group of female chimps and their babies.

parasite An animal that lives on or in another animal and feeds on it.

primate The group of mammals that includes the apes, monkeys, and humans.

stereo vision The ability to see things in three dimensions and judge their distances better.

tropical Found in the tropics, which are the hot areas north and south of the equator.

Further Reading

Books

All About Chimps. Cindy Rodriguez. Vero Beach, FL: Rourke, 2009.

Apes. Carol Ellis. New York: Marshall Cavendish Benchmark, 2011.

Apes and Monkeys. Michael and Jane Pelusey. New York: Marshall Cavendish Benchmark, 2008.

Chimpanzees. Sarah Albee. Pleasantville, NY: Gareth Stevens, 2010.

Chimpanzees. Patricia Davis. Danbury, CT: Grolier, 2009.

Chimpanzees. Jinny Johnson. North Mankato, MD: Smart Apple, 2007.

Chimpanzees. Heidi Moore. Chicago, IL: Heinemann, 2012.

Face to Face with Gorillas. Michael Nicholls. Washington, D.C: National Geographic, 2009.

Monkeys and Apes. Camilla de la Bedoyere. Broomall, PA: Mason Crest, 2009.

Top 50 Reasons to Care about Great Apes. David Barker. Berkeley Heights, NJ: Enslow, 2010.

Websites

Save the Chimps
The world's largest chimpanzee sanctuary.
www.savethechimps.org

National Geographic Chimpanzees
Lots of information about chimpanzees.
http://kids.nationalgeographic.com/kids /animals/creaturefeature/chimpanzee

BBC Nature: Chimps
Videos, news, facts, and photos of chimps.
www.bbc.co.uk/nature/life/Common _Chimpanzee

African Nature Foundation
Information about chimp behavior and habitats, with a photo gallery.
www.awf.org/content/wildlife/detail /chimpanzee

Index